Genius Recipe

The Secret Life of Scones

There's so very much more to this simple recipe
than perhaps you realise!

by Suzy Bowler

Copyright 2014 Suzy Bowler

All Rights Reserved

This book or any portion thereof may not be reproduced or used in any manner whatsoever without the express permission of the publisher except for the use of brief quotations in a book review.

ISBN-13: 978-1515328858

ISBN-10: 1515328856

About the Author

After 14 years running her own restaurants and hotel in Cornwall (in partnership with her sister Maggie) Suzy Bowler started travelling; cooked in a ski resort in the French Alps, on a yacht around Madeira and the Canary Islands, in New Zealand and on a catamaran in the Caribbean before making her home in the British Virgin Islands where she worked as a chef for many years.

Having learned so very much about food and cooking she returned to Cornwall to spend her dotage passing it on (or "sitting on the settee" as her partner calls it!)

suddenlunch.blogspot.co.uk

Also by Suzy Bowler

The Genius Recipes Series

Luscious Ice Creams without a Machine … or much time or effort or having to mash the stuff as it freezes!

Sorbets and Granitas

SOUP (almost) the Only Recipe You'll ever Need

Other Books and eBooks

The Leftovers Handbook: A-Z of Every Ingredient in Your Kitchen with Inspirational Ideas for Using Them

Easy Festive Food for a Stress-Free Christmas

Food for Love: Eat your Way to a Better Sex Life ~ Win/Win Situation!

219 Cooking Tips & Techniques you might find useful!

Easy Ways to Pimp your Food

See all Suzy's books here –
amazon.co.uk/Suzy-Bowler/e/B00AG1YUKE/

Genius Recipes

By "genius recipe" I don't just mean a good idea, I mean the kind of key recipe that can be easily varied to create all sorts of delicious things. In these books I try to explain the principles; the why and how a recipe works, so that you can confidently vary it, add to it and create brilliant dishes of your very own.

In these pages, for instance, I give recipes for sweet and savoury scones, rock cakes, griddle cakes, dumplings, doughnuts and more all based the one simple "genius" recipe. But that's not all! In addition to the straightforward recipes I also make suggestions on how to vary them and having researched different flours, liquids, fats, glazes and toppings I give all the useful information I can think of to help you do this.

The chapters on sweet and on savoury scones are by far the longest as the recipes therein can be adapted to make most of the other things in the book!

This is the fourth in the Genius Recipes series – the first is *"Luscious Ice Creams without a Machine ~ or much time or effort or having to mash the stuff as it freezes!"*. The second is just a booklet really, a companion volume to the ice cream book but concerning sorbets and granitas which, whilst not requiring an ice cream machine, are based on a different genius recipe. Number three is a very useful way of making soup with recipes from leek and potato to Caribbean Callaloo and in each case I give the one key "genius" recipe together with lots of recipes and all the information and help you need to invent your own creations. I have two more on the fire (about a superb way of cooking onions and very useful muffin recipe, but not at the same time).

~ Table of Contents ~

Intro, Info & the Genius Recipe ~ 1

Genius Recipe * Rubbing In * Flours * Fats * Additions * Liquids
9 Important Points * Glazes and Toppings * Storage etc.
Clotted Cream * Cream Teas * American Biscuits * Note

Sweet Scones ~ 10

Traditional Fruit Scones * Rum & Raisin Scones * Hot Cross Scones
Cranberry Orange Scones * Strawberries & Cream Scones
Sautéed Blueberry Scones * Caramelised Apple Scones
Treacle, Golden Syrup, Honey or Maple Syrup Scones * Lemon Poppy Seed Scones
Pecan and Brown Sugar Scones * Sticky Toffee Scones * Peanut Butter Scones
Chocolate Scones * Sticky Orange Buns * Monkey Scones!
Sandwich Scones * Filled Scones

Savoury Scones ~ 19

Cheese Scones with Lots of Variations * Cheddar & Mustard Scones * Herb Scones
Sweet Potato Scones * Caramelised Onion Scones & Likky Cakes
Garlic Bread Scones * Roasted Garlic Scones * Black Garlic Scones!
Sautéed Mushrooms Scones * Roasted Tomato Scones * Panko Crusted Balls

No Oven – No Problem! ~ 26

Griddle aka Girdle Scones * Not Quite Drop Scones!
Flatbreads

Shortcakes ~ 29

Almost Classic Strawberry Shortcake * Caramel-Banana Shortcakes
Tomato Shortcakes

Rock Cakes aka Rock Buns ~ 31

Traditional Rock Cakes * Fully Loaded Fruit and Nut Rock Cakes
Dried Cherry & White Chocolate Rock Cakes
Dark Chocolate (and Chilli) Rock Cakes
Caribbean Coconut Rock Cakes * Gingerbread Rock Cakes

Regional Variations ~ 34

Northumbrian Singin' Hinnies * Welsh Cakes * Sussex Plum Heavies
Lardy Johns * Fat Rascals * Devonshire Apple Dappy

Cobblers, Slumps & Similar 39

Cobblers * Plum Cobbler * Slumps aka Grunts
Pandowdy

Short & Crumbly ~ 42

Tarts * How to Bake Blind * Rustic Tarts
Tarte Tatin * Caramelised Shallot Tatin with Blue Cheese Crust
Pies * Turnovers * Biscuits of the English Persuasion * Crumble

Dumplings & Doughnuts ~ 47

Dumplings * Likky Stew with a Natterjack * Sweet Dumplings
Grand-Père * Doughnuts * Savoury Doughnuts * Suggestions

Leftovers! ~ 51

Dough Trimmings * Leftovers Scones and Similar
Scone and (no) Butter Pudding * Leftover Dumplings

5 Ancillary Recipes ~ 55

Sticky Toffee Sauce * Alcohol Soaked Fruit
Drops Scones as we normally understand them!
Sausage Gravy! * How to Roast Garlic

Summing Up ~ 59

Index ~ 60

Q. What's the fastest cake in the World?
A. Scone

... but only if you pronounce it "correctly" to sound like "it's gone", seemingly a lot of people rhyme it with stone and for them, very sadly, this joke doesn't work.

~ *Intro, Info & the Genius Recipe* ~

I had a lot of experience with scones when my sister and I owned a seaside hotel and restaurant in Cornwall, we sold hundreds of the buggers. Our Cornish Cream Teas were very good even though I do say so myself; clotted cream from the farm up the road, a choice of jams in generous bowls and warm, fresh out the oven (we baked constantly all afternoon and still had trouble keeping up) really large homemade scones.

> **Cream Teas 2.45**
> ...you may blush at the size of our scones!

It was not until I left Cornwall, however, and had time to play around a bit that I realised the full potential of this humble recipe and it has served me very well ever since.

It turns out that this might just be the most useful dough in the world! Not only can it be varied to create any sweet or savoury scone, American biscuit, griddle cake or rock bun you can think of, not only is it the base recipe for many traditional and ancient dishes but it also make lovely fluffy dumplings, crisp doughnuts, cobblers, turnovers, pie crust (nicer than pastry, I think, as it's so short and crumbly) and more.

Genius Recipe

Makes 6-8 normal sized scones or 4 embarrassingly large ones, the recipe can easily be doubled.

225g/8oz self-raising flour
OR
225g/8oz plain flour + 1 rounded teaspoon baking powder (about 8g/scant ½oz)
a pinch of salt
60g/2½oz cold butter or margarine
25g/1oz caster sugar
100ml/3½ fl oz milk

~ Preheat the oven to 200°C/400°F/180C fan/gas 6.
~ Stir together the flour, salt and baking powder (if using).
~ Add the butter or margarine and "rub in" with your fingers until a breadcrumb tex-

ture is achieved (see below).
~ Stir in the sugar once you have finished rubbing in; if you add it earlier it's uncomfortable on the hands although, of course, it does exfoliate.
~ Add the milk and mix in, by hand is easiest, add a little more milk if too dry or a little more flour if too wet – work just enough to form a soft dough.
~ On a floured surface press or roll the dough out to about 1¼cm/½" thick and using a cookie cutter cut into rounds. Or you could cut into squares which are easier and more economical on time: no re-rolling. They look quite good too.
~ Transfer the scones to a greased baking tray, brush their tops with a little milk and bake in the oven till risen and golden – about 15 minutes.
~ Transfer to a cooling rack till needed.

Scones are best served slightly warm with clotted cream and jam for a traditional cream tea or, of course, with anything you like, they're your scones.

Rubbing In

This is just lightly rubbing the flour and the fat between your fingertips till the mixture resembles breadcrumbs.

~ If you use butter cut it up into small pieces first for easier rubbing in, margarine being softer doesn't need this.
~ Hold your hands a little above the bowl so that the flour and fat stays cool, airy and flaky. Be gentle with it!
~ Shake the bowl occasionally which will cause larger pieces of fat to be revealed ready for further rubbing in.

You can also do this in a food processor using the pulse button, but it hardly seems worth the faff for a few scones or whatever. It is quick and easy and more controllable by hand.

Flours

~ Plain flour (all purpose flour in America) plus baking powder is my preference.
~ Self raising flour is fine so long as it is fresh. Be warned that in America self-rising flour, as it is known there, often also contains salt so act accordingly. I personally don't really see much point in buying self-raising when I can just add leavening to plain flour.
~ Cake flour is excellent for soft and tender scones.
~ Bread flour is not appropriate as it is high in gluten which is something we are trying to avoid in this dough.

~ Wholemeal flour – this make tasty but slightly heavier scones. A cunning ruse is to use plain flour but pat or roll the dough out on wholemeal for a pretty and healthy looking finish.

Fats

~ Butter is, generally speaking, the most delicious fat to use for these recipes but as it is hard when cold the rubbing in is slightly strenuous! One way round this is to chill the butter very thorough, coarsely grate it and stir through the dry ingredients.

Another way to incorporate the butter is to add small butter nuggets to the flour, make the dough immediately without further rubbing in and then treat it like puff pastry. Roll the dough out on a lightly floured board, fold in in three (letter fold), repeat and then continue as usual. This results in deliciously flaky scones which are well worth the extra effort.

~ Margarine is easier to work with; it is an ideal consistency for rubbing in so nice and quick. I also think that the results are a little lighter and fluffier than butter scones but not quite so delicious.
~ Lard is a possibility and would certainly have been used in traditional recipes such as Fat Rascals, Welsh Cakes and, of course, Lardy Johns – see page 34 for the chapter on regional recipes.
~ Cream cheese makes for a slightly heavier scone but, depending on the cream cheese, with a good flavour; Boursin or similar is a great choice.

Additions

As you will be able to tell, reading this book, all sorts of things can be added to this wonderful dough. Go wild but there are just a few things to bear in mind ...

~ Stir in any additions after you have rubbed in the fat and flour and before adding the liquid, it's easier that way.
~ Don't overload the dough; 75g/3oz of additions is about right for this quantity.
~ When adding anything wet, juicy or oily be cautious with the milk or other liquid as the dough will already be a little moist.

Liquids

I stipulate milk in the key recipe and this works very well indeed. There are other options though and, like the good cookbook writer I am, I have tested assiduously.

My findings? In short, they all work! In more detail …

~ Buttermilk – in America buttermilk is the preferred liquid for biscuits but this is not so easily acquired in the UK. If you can't get any a squeeze of lemon juice in the milk can be a good substitute. I found these to be maybe a little lighter but probably not worth cutting into a lemon!
~ Cream – lovely, as one would expect; crisp and fragile crust, tender crumb, rich taste.
~ Sour Cream – I couldn't taste much difference to those made with double cream; maybe a slightly cheesy flavour. Lovely crust again.
~ Yogurt – light pleasant tang to it. I added some almonds for identification purposes!

~ Coconut Milk – I used the thick milk at the top of the tin (open carefully without shaking the can first), it gave soft scones and a slight coconutty flavour, but I do mean slight. Next time I might add a drop or two of rum and some lime zest or similar!

~ Coffee – use good strong coffee and they will taste great, they are light and crispy and excellent with chopped chocolate mixed into the dough. Light brown sugar is good instead of caster in these and drip or two of vanilla extract is nice.

~ Stock! – obviously this depends on what stock; I used some light vegetable broth and freshly chopped parsley. These would be good with soup or to make dumplings – details on page 48.

~ Spicy Tomato Pasta Sauce!! – a last minute thought which was delicious! Next time maybe I'll add some cheese to the mix.

~ Water works too in a bland sort of way but we can all do better than that (except when making Lardy Johns, page 37).

9 Important Points

1. Baking powder must be fresh and dry or it won't work. If you've had it more than say 6 months or if it is hard and stuck together buy a new batch.
2. Fat and liquid must be cold, straight from the fridge is best, cooked fruits or other additions must also be cold. Even cold hands are a good idea.
3. Add liquid tentatively – flours are differently absorbent and other ingredients may contribute moisture; add about half of the milk (or other liquid) at first and then the rest gradually till a soft workable dough is achieved.
4. Handle the dough as little as possible for a tender result. Work quickly just until the ingredients are combined, the dough need not be smooth. I use my hands but a fork or palette knife works well too.
5. I usually pat the dough into shape rather than roll it, try to get as many scones as possible out of the first patting/rolling so as to not work it too much.
6. Be firm and direct when cutting the dough, don't twist the cutter or knife or you could get wonky scones and they might not rise so well.
7. Scones that are a bit crowded on the baking tray tend to rise more as they help each other. Separate them gently when cooked, they will have soft edges. If you'd rather have crisper edges bake them farther apart.
8. The scones are cooked when risen and golden and if you tap them on their bottoms they sound hollow.
9. I considered including cup measurements to the recipes but I find this a little inaccurate (and I do know of which I speak have worked in the Americas!), investing in scales is a good idea if you take baking seriously.

Glazes and Toppings

~ Milk and cream add a soft sheen, beaten egg a glossier one and just egg yolk a very rich golden glaze.
~ Don't let any dribble down sides of scones as this might hinder their rising.
~ A sprinkling of sugar on top of the glaze before baking gives a nice crunchy topping – or try coarse sea salt on savoury scones.
~ Streusel topping – rub together 25g/1oz each plain flour and softened butter and then stir in 25g/1oz sugar. Brush the scones with butter and then sprinkle with the mix before baking.
~ If glazing when fresh out the oven remember that some will be absorbed by the hot scones and choose something delicious. So as not to make a mess put the scones on a cooling rack and stand it on some foil or a baking tray to catch the drips.
~ Drizzle cooled scones with a little icing.
~ A simple dusting of icing/confectioner's sugar works well too.

Storage etc.

~ The dry ingredients and fat can be mixed in advance and kept in the fridge, just add the milk or other liquid at the last minute before cooking. In fact it's a good idea if you are prone to making this sort of thing to keep a bag of the mixture in the freezer to use as and when you need it.
~ The prepared uncooked scones can actually be frozen on baking trays and then decanted into an airtight bag and stored in the freezer till needed. Cook them from frozen just adding a few more minutes to the baking time.

~ Scones and their friends and relations are best served fresh and preferably still warm from the oven.

~ If you must keep them for a while make sure they are completely cold, then put a couple of sheets of kitchen roll in an airtight container, place the scones on top and seal. They are OK for a couple of days like this.

~ Cooked scones freeze very well, thaw before reheating.

~ Reheat in a moderate oven, 180°C/350°F/160°C fan/gas 4-ish, for about 5 minutes or (although I'm not a great fan of them) in a microwave for a few seconds, to just warm through. The oven will give a nicer finish with a crisp crust.

~ Scones toast beautifully.

Cream Teas

Clotted Cream is luscious, rich, 55% butterfat, utterly delicious cream. I don't think it's available in the US except in jars which in no way equals the wonderful real thing, so don't bother unless you can get genuine fresh clotted cream, use whipped cream instead.

In Cornwall we do as nature intended; the jam is spread onto the scone first and then topped with clotted cream. I believe they do things differently in other parts of the country.

There is, however, a mathematical formula for creating the perfect cream tea. Dr. Cheng, a mathematician at the University of Sheffield's School of Mathematics and Statistics did some research on the subject and came up with the following info …

~ Jam, due to its density, needs to be spread prior to the application of the clotted cream. Putting it on after the cream may cause the jam to run off – creating sticky fingers.

~ The thickness of the cream should also not be thicker than the scone, as the scone will become off balance whilst trying to eat it.

~ If r is the radius of the scone, then we have the following formula for the thickness of the jam and the thickness of the cream.

$$\text{thickness of clotted cream} = \frac{r^3}{8(r-1)^2}$$

$$\text{thickness of jam} = \frac{3r^3}{40(r-\frac{1}{2})^2}$$

Obvious when you think about it!

A word on American Biscuits

American chaps call our scones biscuits. To complicate matters further they call biscuits cookies and they also actually have scones but, unlike ours, they are larger, triangular and fancier – iced or drizzled, which is not necessarily a bad thing. Sometimes, particularly in the south, Americans use buttermilk instead of whole milk in their biscuits but, quite frequently, they don't!

Until I became friends with real bona fide Americans I was always bemused by the thought of biscuits with gravy. What a pervie idea! What sort of biscuits? Surely not Custard Creams! Even now, understanding to an extent the American concept of biscuits, it still seems a little strange but I suppose it's OK – just like serving a dry dumpling!

Of course, putting the gravy question to one side for a moment (the recipe is on page 57), some American biscuits are very good indeed.

Note ...

As all the recipes in the book are based on this one key recipe I don't keep repeating it, I just say "*1 x key recipe*" or "*make the basic recipe*" or similar. This means the book isn't padded out with unnecessary repetitions and luckily the key recipe is so simple and genius I don't think it will be a problem.

~ *Sweet Scones* ~

Traditional Fruit Scones

Easy peasy, just add about 75g/3oz of dried fruit of your choice to the key recipe when adding the sugar. I like golden sultanas best, but what I really, really like best are ...

Rum & Raisin Scones

This may just be because I've spent many years living in the Caribbean. Probably you wouldn't like them one little bit but just in case you want to give them a go think about it a few days ahead and make some Alcohol Soaked Fruit first – page 56.

As with the Fruit Scones above you need to add 75g/3oz of alcoholic fruit (raisins in rum to stick to the theme) at the same time as you add the sugar. I wouldn't be too pernickety about draining the fruit when lifting it out of the rum; but do add the milk very sparingly and tentatively as the rum from the fruit will have already wetted the dough a little.

For best results it is especially important to eat alcoholic scones whilst still warm.

Hot Cross Scones

Make the fruit scones above (not the alcoholic ones as that might be blasphemous!) BUT with the following adjustments ...

~ Add ½ teaspoon of mixed spice to the flour at the start of the recipe.
~ Use soft light brown sugar instead of caster sugar.
~ Use mixed fruit which includes mixed peel.

Glaze ...

~ Gently melt together 1 tablespoon of caster sugar and the juice of half an orange.
~ Brush over the hot cross scones whilst still warm.

3 ways to make the crosses ...

1. Make a smooth dough by mixing together 25g/1oz plain flour and one tablespoon of water. Roll out thinly and cut into strips. Make crosses on top of the scones before baking.
2. Cut strips of marzipan and stick on top of the cooked buns immediately after glazing. Flash under a hot grill, watching constantly, to brown the marzipan.
3. Use icing or melted chocolate to pipe crosses onto cooked, cooled scones.

Cranberry & Orange Scones

Grate the zest from the orange (just the brightly coloured bit – none of the bitter white under it) BEFORE you juice the orange; it is so much easier that way.

> finely grated zest of a lovely orange
> the juice of the same orange, divided in two
> 75g/3oz dried cranberries
> 1 x key recipe
> 1 tablespoon caster sugar

~ Prepare the orange zest and juice.
~ Stir the cranberries into half the orange juice (the other half is for the glaze) and set aside to steep – up to 24 hours is fine.
~ Preheat the oven to 200°C/400°F/180C fan/gas 6.
~ Make the basic recipe adding the fruit and their juices plus the zest together with the sugar.
~ Add enough milk to form a soft workable dough – this will be a lot less milk than usual because of the orange juice.
~ Cut into scones and place on a lightly greased baking tray.
~ Bake till risen and golden.
~ Whilst they are cooking stir together the other half of the orange juice and the tablespoon of caster sugar.
~ Glaze the scones with this when they have been out of the oven a few minutes.

If you want to put a splash of Cointreau or other orange liqueur in with the orange juice when soaking the cranberries, well … I couldn't possible comment.

Fresh fruit can also be added to the mix; coarsely chop if necessary, which it isn't with blueberries for instance, or grate as in the case of apples. Stir the fruit in with the sugar and be a little careful when adding the milk as the fruit will add its own moisture.

Strawberries & Cream Scones

The strawberry juices make the scones look very golden and wholesome but don't be fooled!

> 1 x key recipe made with cream
> 100g/3½oz strawberries – hulled and coarsely chopped

~ Preheat the oven to 200°C/400°F/180C fan/gas 6.
~ Make the basic recipe adding the fruit and their juices with the sugar.
~ Add just enough cream to form a soft workable dough – this will be less than usual.

- ~ Cut into scones and place on a lightly greased baking tray.
- ~ Bake till risen and golden.

Alternatively purée the strawberries and add to the flour mixture together with the milk – pretty pink scones!

Sautéed Blueberry Scones

75g/3oz fresh blueberries
a knob of butter
1 tablespoon caster sugar
1 x key recipe

- ~ Sauté the berries together with the butter and sugar until they start to burst.
- ~ Set aside and cool completely.
- ~ Preheat the oven to 200°C/400°F/180C fan/gas 6.
- ~ Make the dough adding the cooked fruit and juices before the milk and then adding just enough milk to make a soft workable dough.
- ~ Roll or pat the dough out, cut into scones and bake for about 15 minutes till risen and golden.

Caramelised Apple Scones

1 x key recipe
1 crisp eating apple
55g/2oz butter
1 tablespoon caster sugar

- ~ Peel the apple and cut in about 5mm/¼" dice.
- ~ Melt the 55g/2oz butter and sauté the apple till it is starting to soften and turn colour.
- ~ Stir in the sugar and cook, stirring gently, till the sugar has melted and caramelised in the butter.
- ~ Cool.
- ~ Preheat the oven to 200°C/400°F/180C fan/gas 6.
- ~ Make the scones as usual, stirring in the cool apple and its juices before adding any liquid and then do so carefully as the dough will already be moist from the apples.
- ~ Bake till gorgeous!

Treacle, Golden Syrup, Honey or Maple Syrup Scones

1 x key recipe – without the sugar
2 tablespoons of your chosen syrup
25g/1oz butter
2 more tablespoons of your chosen syrup

~ Preheat the oven to 200°C/400°F/180C fan/gas 6.
~ Make the key recipe adding the syrup at the same time as the milk and being tentative with the milk until you see how the dough is coming on.
~ Bake till risen and golden.
~ Meanwhile gently melt together the remaining butter and syrup to make a glaze.
~ As soon as the scones are out of the oven brush with half the glaze, wait 10 minutes or so and glaze again.

Additions – lemon zest or almonds are good with honey, ginger is nice with golden syrup and pecans or crunchy bits of bacon are a good addition to the maple syrup scones. Dried fruits and/or a pinch of cinnamon go well with treacle or add ground ginger, cinnamon and maybe cloves to make gingerbread scones!

Lemon Poppy Seed Scones

Good served with just clotted cream and, perhaps, a little lemon curd although this may be gilding the lily. Orange Poppy Seed Scones are good too!

1 x key recipe
1 lovely big juicy lemon or 2 smaller ones
2 tablespoons poppy seeds
an extra tablespoon of sugar

~ Preheat the oven to 200°C/400°F/180C fan/gas 6.
~ Finely grate the zest from lemons – this is just the yellow outside, don't grate the white pith under the yellow; it is bitter.
~ Squeeze the juice and divide into two halves.
~ When making the dough add the poppy seeds and the lemon zest together with the sugar.
~ Use half the lemon juice as part of the liquid then add the milk or cream till you have a soft workable dough
~ Roll, cut and bake the scones till risen and golden.
~ Whilst the scones are baking stir the other tablespoon of sugar into the rest of the lemon juice.
~ As soon as the scones are ready and out of the oven brush their tops with the lemon

syrup and keep brushing it on till it is all gone – the hot scones will absorb it deliciously leaving a sugary crust.

Pecan and Brown Sugar Scones

1 x key recipe using soft light brown sugar
55g/2oz lightly toasted and coarsely chopped pecans

~ Preheat the oven to 200°C/400°F/180C fan/gas 6.
~ Make and bake the scones as usual but using the soft light brown sugar instead of white and kneading in the chopped nuts after adding the milk.

Sticky Toffee Scones

1 x key recipe using soft light brown sugar
75g/3oz coarsely chopped dates
2 or 3 tablespoons Sticky Toffee Sauce – see page 55

~ Preheat the oven to 200°C/400°F/180C fan/gas 6.
~ Make the scones as usual adding the dates to the dry ingredients before the milk.
~ Bake till perfect then place on a rack which is in turn placed on a tray or sheet of paper or something capable of catching drips.
~ Allow to cool for 10 minutes or so then drizzle with the sauce.
~ Cool.

Peanut Butter Scones

This is an unusual variation which I tried on the spur of the moment and it worked, the scones have a lovely texture (and taste good too, of course)!

1 x key recipe BUT …
replace the white sugar with soft light brown sugar
replace the butter with peanut butter!!

~ Just act as normal! I used crunchy peanut butter but I am sure smooth would work just as well!

Note – I used bought in peanut butter, homemade or organic is much oilier and may not work.

Chocolate Scones

1 x key recipe – slight modified thus …
replace 75g/3oz of the flour with cocoa
use soft light brown sugar
stir 1 teaspoon vanilla extract into the milk

~ Proceed as usual.

Good additions would be grated orange zest and/or chocolate chips.

Sticky Orange Buns

55g/2oz butter plus a little extra
1 tablespoon finely grated orange zest
120ml/4 fl oz orange juice
100g/3½ oz soft light brown sugar
1 x key recipe
another 55g/2oz soft light brown sugar
½ teaspoon ground cinnamon

~ Preheat the oven to 200°C/400°F/180C fan/gas 6.
~ Grease a shallow ovenproof dish (a 20cm/8" square baking pan would be ideal) with the extra butter.
~ Melt together the 55g/2oz of butter, the orange zest, orange juice and sugar.
~ Pour into the greased pan and brush up the sides.
~ Make the key recipe and roll out to a large rectangle about ½cm/¼" thick.
~ Mix together the rest of the sugar and the cinnamon and sprinkle over the dough.
~ Roll up from a long edge and cut into slices about 2¼cm/1" thick.
~ Place the slices cut side down in the baking pan spaced slightly apart as they will rise sideways!
~ Bake till risen and golden.
~ Immediately and very carefully turn out onto a large plate – the juices will be sticky and caramelised in places but could still burn you!
~ Serve warm.

Monkey Scones!

1 x key recipe
½ teaspoon vanilla extract
40g/1½oz butter
40g/1½oz soft light brown sugar

~ Preheat the oven to 200°C/400°F/180C fan/gas 6.
~ Make the dough adding the vanilla together with the milk.
~ Melt together the butter and sugar and the easiest way to do this is to put them in the shallow ovenproof dish you intend to use for baking and pop it in the oven for a few minutes.
~ Roll the dough into walnut sized balls.
~ Stir together the melted butter and sugar.
~ Turn each little ball of dough in the sugary goo and arrange in a pile so that they stick together in places.
~ Bake for about 15-20 minutes till risen and firm and golden.
~ Cool till comfortable to touch by hand and serve in the pile so that people can help themselves.

These are also good using honey or maple syrup but I love the butterscotch flavour with the crunchiness of the sugar.

Sandwich Scones

1x key recipe
2-3 tablespoons jam or marmalade or maybe Nutella!

~ Preheat the oven to 200°C/400°F/180C fan/gas 6.
~ Make the dough and roll or pat it out half as thick as usual.
~ Spread the jam on half of the dough and fold over the other half.
~ Press lightly into place and cut your scones.
~ Bake as usual.

Filled Scones

Divide dough into scone sized balls and put a nugget of something appropriate in the middle of each one. Reform the dough totally enclosing the filling and flatten into something closely resembling a scone. Bake as usual.

Chocolate is good in plain sweet scones and others, marzipan in fruit and/or nut scones and different cheeses in savoury scones.

~ *Savoury Scones* ~

Simply put leave the sugar out of the key recipe and up the salt slightly, then follow one of these recipes, or make one up!

Cheese Scones

"Cheese Scones" doesn't do justice to the huge range of scones that can be made by varying the cheese and other additions.

1 x key recipe – no sugar
75g/3oz cheese of your choice – grated or crumbled or coarsely chopped

~ Preheat the oven to 200°C/400°F/180C fan/gas 6.
~ Make the dough mixing in the cheese after rubbing in the fat.
~ Add any other ingredients and seasonings.
~ Mix to a soft workable dough with the milk.
~ Roll or pat out the dough, cut to shape and place on a lightly greased baking tray.
~ Maybe, if you feel like it, brush with butter or cream and sprinkle with a little extra cheese and/or sea salt.
~ Bake for 15 minutes-ish till risen, golden and with hollow sounding botties.

Easy cheese-enhancing things to add to these scones are a pinch of cayenne or mustard powder or maybe a teaspoon of Marmite stirred into the liquid.

Cheddar & Mustard Scones

I always use lovely crumbly extra mature Cornish Crackler, it is everything a Cheddar cheese should be and more.

Add a generous pinch of mustard powder to flour and replace some of the milk with 1½ tablespoons of wholegrain mustard.

Here are some more ideas:

~ Cheddar with hot chilli flakes.
~ Cheddar and crumbled crispy bacon.
~ Try smoked cheddar.
~ Blue cheese with loads of black pepper.
~ Blue cheese and toasted walnuts.
~ Brie (freeze then dice it), dried cranberries and bacon.
~ Firm goat cheese and dried figs.
~ Grated Parmesan and a spoonful of pesto (a little less milk needed here).
~ Swiss cheese and Parma ham.
~ Your turn!

Not So Cheesy Scones

Although it works really well cheese is not the only possibility for a savoury scone.

Herb Scones

In short add a 2 or 3 tablespoons of fresh herbs to the dough before adding the liquid. If you only have dried herbs then you need much less as they are very strong, say 1 teaspoon per batch.

Try sage with caramelised onions (page 21), rosemary in garlic scones (page 22), lavender in honey scones (page 14), lemon and parsley and so on.

Sweet Potato Scones

Pumpkin also works well in this recipe.

> 1 x key recipe – no sugar
> a little extra salt
> 100g/3½oz mashed cooked sweet potato (or pumpkin)
> a few chilli flakes or a drop of hot sauce – optional

~ Preheat the oven to 200°C/400°F/180C fan/gas 6.
~ Make the basic recipe adding the mashed sweet potato and seasoning before adding the milk.
~ Add just enough milk to form a soft workable dough – this will be less than usual.
~ Cut into scones and place on a lightly greased baking tray.
~ Bake till risen and golden – about 15 minutes.

Caramelised Onion Scones & Likky Cakes

> 1 medium onion or small leek
> a knob of butter
> a little salt
> 1 x key recipe – no sugar

- Thinly slice the onion or leek.
- Melt the butter in a small pan with a lid.
- Stir in the onion or leek and season lightly.
- Press a piece of foil or a butter wrapper directly onto the onion/leek to cover completely.
- Turn down the heat, put the lid on and cook very gently till the onion/leek are very tender.
- Allow to cool.
- Make the scones as usual adding the cooked onion/leek before the milk and adding the milk abstemiously.

3 Garlic Scones

Garlic Bread Scones

Simply use garlic butter as the fat in the key recipe, don't glaze with anything but when fresh out the oven brush the tops with little more garlic butter. Grated Parmesan would be good in these too.

Roasted Garlic Scones

1 x key recipe – no sugar
1 head of roasted garlic – see page 57

- Preheat the oven to 200°C/400°F/180C fan/gas 6.
- Make the basic recipe squeezing in the lovely soft roasted garlic before adding the milk.
- Carefully add enough milk to form a soft workable dough – this will be less than usual.
- Cut into scones and place on a lightly greased baking tray.
- Bake till risen and golden – about 15 minutes.

Black Garlic Scones!

This is another spur of the moment idea brought on by having a jar of black garlic paste to play with. Black Garlic is a wonderful "new" ingredient; aged garlic which is sweet and molasses-ish with very little garlic flavour, actually. I urge you to look out for the whole garlic and the paste; if you like food I don't think you'll regret it!

These are delicious with blue cheese and red wine.

1 x key recipe – no sugar
6 cloves of black garlic coarsely chopped OR 1½ teaspoons of paste

~ Proceed as usual adding the chopped garlic after the rubbing in or the paste together with the milk.

Sautéed Mushroom Scones

1 tablespoon of olive oil
120g/4oz mushrooms
1 finely minced clove of garlic OR 1 teaspoon of finely chopped onion – both optional
1 x key recipe – no sugar
1 tablespoon finely chopped parsley

~ Slice the mushrooms, select 1 pretty mushroom slice per scone.
~ Chop the rest of the mushrooms and sauté (including the pretty slices) in the olive oil till turning brown.
~ Set the slices aside and stir in the garlic or onion if using, remove from heat and set aside to cool.
~ When making the scones add the chopped mushrooms, their juices and the parsley before the milk which you will then add a little at a time to make sure the dough is not too wet.
~ Top each scone with a mushroom slice and bake as usual.

Roasted Tomato Scones

1 x key recipe – just a touch of sugar!
120g/4oz whole cherry or baby plum tomatoes
1 tablespoon of olive oil

~ Preheat the oven to 200°C/400°F/180C fan/gas 6.
~ Toss the tomatoes with the olive oil, season to taste and cook for 15-20 minutes till squishy and collapsed.
~ Cool.
~ Proceed with the scones as normal using the roasted tomatoes and their juices as the liquid and topping up with milk as necessary.

Two good additions to these are a pinch of cayenne and/or some grated Parmesan.

Other savoury suggestions …

~ Lots of freshly and coarsely ground black pepper.
~ Lemon zest and parsley or dill – split and fill with sour cream and smoked salmon.
~ Bacon or ham or chorizo.
~ Sweet Chilli Scones – add 1 teaspoon of sweet chilli sauce together with the liquid. Grated lime zest would a good further addition and, incidentally, these are lovely with seafood!
~ Parmesan, basil and pine nuts.
~ Crunchy bacon pieces and a maple syrup glaze.
~ Sautéed onion, red pepper and garlic with a pinch of chilli.
~ Sundried tomatoes, chopped olives and Feta.

Panko Crusted Balls!

Roll scone dough into small balls and then roll in panko crumbs pressing lightly to coat. Bake as usual and serve as nibbles or to dip in things! They are lovely and crunchy

~ *No Oven – No Problem!* ~

This is just a short chapter because it is eminently possible to cook all of the above scones on top of the stove.

Griddle aka Girdle Scones

Simply pat or roll the dough out about 1½cm/½" thick, cut to desired shape and cook 3-4 minutes per side on a lightly greased griddle or sturdy frying pan.

They are as good as baked. As an example here is the same dough (Blue Cheese & Black Pepper) cooked in the oven and on the griddle; the wedge was baked, the round scone was cooked on top of the stove.

Not Quite Drop Scones!

Alternatively if you make the dough a little on the wet side and spoon dollops of the batter onto the hot griddle you get drop scones but not quite as we know them, Jim!

~ Use a little more oil than usual which will make them crisper.
~ As soon as they have landed in the pan flatten them out slightly with the back of a spoon.
~ Cook for 4-5minutes per side till risen and crisp and golden.

To avoid disappointment, the recipe for our normal perception of drop scones is on page 56.

Flatbreads

~ Roll your chosen version of the dough out thinly.
~ Aim for a round-ish shape but I think flatbreads (including pizzas) look more attractive and homemade if they are bit asymmetrical.
~ Heat a frying pan and oil it lightly.
~ Add the flatbread and cook over medium heat, turning once, till golden on both sides.
~ Eat whilst still warm.

Incidentally – sweet doughs make interestingly different flat breads to serve with fruit, for instance!

~ *Shortcakes* ~

Another very scone-like creature, only more luxurious, is the shortcake. The luxuriousness is achieved firstly by using cream instead of milk in the key recipe then by adding sumptuous fillings. Just a few examples here, use your imagination!

Almost Classic Strawberry Shortcake – makes 4

The filling for this is fresh strawberries turned in a little caster sugar together with homemade Clotted Cream Ice Cream – the incredibly easy no-churn, no faff recipe for which is in *"Luscious Ice Creams without a Machine "*.

1 x key recipe using cream
a little extra sugar for sprinkling
450g/1lb fresh strawberries
2 tablespoons caster sugar
150ml/5 fl oz vanilla ice cream
(if you haven't yet made the clotted cream version)

~ Stem and slice the strawberries and toss with the 2 tablespoons of sugar. Set aside in the fridge till needed.
~ Preheat the oven to 200°C/400°F/180C fan/gas 6.
~ Make the scones, brush tops with milk and then sprinkle with a little sugar.
~ Bake till gorgeous.
~ When baked cool to room temperature.
~ To serve split the scones, add a generous scoop of ice cream to each scone bottom, top with sliced strawberries and put on the lid.

For the classic version fill with 150ml/5 fl oz double (heavy) cream whipped with a tablespoon of icing sugar and ½ teaspoon of vanilla extract.

Caramel-Banana Shortcakes

By the way I can't abide bananas and am gutted that scientists say we are so closely related sharing, as we do, some 60% of our DNA. However a lot of people seem to take pleasure in a banana so I often cook with them and am reliably informed that this is delicious.

Makes 4.

1 x key recipe made with cream
a little extra sugar for sprinkling
2 ripe bananas
1 tablespoon light brown sugar
2 tablespoons rum
100ml/3½ fl oz double (heavy) cream
100ml/3½ fl oz Sticky Toffee Sauce (see page 55) at room temperature

~ Preheat the oven to 200°C/400°F/180C fan/gas 6.
~ Make the scones, brush tops with milk and then sprinkle with a little sugar.
~ Bake till gorgeous.
~ When baked cool to room temperature.
~ Meanwhile peel and slice the bananas and toss with the light brown sugar and the rum. Set aside till needed.
~ Whisk the cream till thick.
~ To assemble split the scones and spread each base, generously, with Sticky Toffee Sauce.
~ Top sauce with macerated bananas and drizzle over any sugary rum that is left.
~ Top bananas with whipped cream
~ Top whipped cream with sugary scone top.

Tomato Shortcakes

Basically cheese scones filled with cream cheese (preferably lightened with a little double cream) and tomatoes tossed with red onion and herbs. Voila – a savoury cream tea!

~ *Rock Cakes aka Rock Buns* ~

Now yer rock cake (or rock bun) is very like yer actual scone except that an egg (plus some milk) is used to bind the dough and each little cake is formed into a rock-resembling dollop rather than a neat little cake. Rock cakes cake take more additions, up to 150g/6oz.

Traditional Rock Cakes

1 x key recipe BUT replace the milk with …
1 egg beaten with 2 tablespoons milk
150g/6oz dried fruit
1 teaspoon mixed spice
a little extra sugar for sprinkling

~ Preheat the oven to 200°C/400°F/180C fan/gas 6.
~ Make the basic dough stirring the dried fruit in with the sugar.
~ Mix to a soft dough with the egg and milk – you may need a little more milk depending on the size of the egg and the dryness of the flour.
~ Gently form into 6-8 rugged buns, place on a lightly greased baking tray and sprinkle with sugar.
~ Bake for about 15 minutes till risen, crusty and touched with gold.

Fully Loaded Fruit and Nut Rock Cakes

As above only using 75g/3oz each coarsely chopped nuts and dried fruit of choice.

Dried Cherry & White Chocolate Rock Cakes

As above but replace the dried fruit with …

75g/3oz coarsely chopped white chocolate
75g/3oz dried cherries

… and replace the mixed spice with ½ teaspoon vanilla extract.

Dark Chocolate (and Chilli) Rock Cakes

Same again only …

150g/6oz dark chocolate coarsely chopped
a pinch of dried chilli flakes – optional and to taste

Alternatively you could use dark chilli chocolate.

Caribbean Coconut Rock Cakes

1 x key recipe using soft light brown sugar and
replace the milk with 1 egg beaten with 2 tablespoons milk
75g/3oz raisins (quite possibly the rum soaked ones in the recipe on page 56)
¼ teaspoon nutmeg (freshly grated if possible)
½ teaspoon ground cinnamon
55g/2oz shredded or desiccated coconut
a little extra soft light brown sugar for sprinkling

The same method again, of course, but if you use the rum soaked fruit do be a little cautious when adding the milk and egg as the dough will already be a little moist.

Gingerbread Rock Cakes

1 x key recipe using soft dark brown sugar and
replace the milk with 1 egg beaten with 2 tablespoons milk
75g/3oz coarsely chopped crystallised ginger OR stem ginger from the jar
1½ teaspoons ground ginger
½ teaspoon ground cinnamon

Same again but if using stem ginger bear in mind, when adding the milk, that it will have already added some moisture to the mix

If using stem ginger it might be a good idea to use a little of the syrup to glaze the rock cakes when they come out the oven.

Get the picture?

~ *Regional Variations* ~

This must be a fairly obvious dough recipe as it has evolved in various forms all over the place.

Northumbrian Singin' Hinnies

My love interest who is a Geordie lad first described 'Singin' Hinnies' to me, a dish from Up North; a sort of scone, often fruited which is cooked on top of the stove.

Traditionally they were cooked in animal fat, preferably lamb oddly enough, and the sound of the fat melting on the griddle made a singing sound. "Hinnie" is a Northumbrian term of endearment as, apparently, is "fatty", "poopants" and "you big woofus".

1 x key recipe
75g/3oz dried fruit – optional, I don't usually bother

~ Make the dough.
~ Pat it into a freeform circle about 1¼cm/½" thick and cut into wedges.
~ Heat a griddle or frying pan till good and hot and rub with a piece of lamb fat or a little oil.
~ Lay the hinnies in the pan, slightly separated, and cook gently till their bottoms are golden – 3-4 minutes.
~ Turn and cook the other sides the same.
~ Serve immediately with butter and honey or whatever you fancy.

Welsh Cakes ~ Pice ar y maen

1 x key recipe BUT to be traditional at least half the fat should be lard
1 egg – beaten
75g/3oz currants
½ teaspoon mixed spice
1 tablespoon caster sugar

~ When making the basic recipe add the currants and mixed spice with the sugar.
~ Next add the egg and finally just enough milk to make a soft workable dough.
~ Preheat your griddle or heavy pan, grease lightly with a little oil.
~ Whilst it is heating roll or pat the dough out to about 1¼cm/½" thick and cut into rounds.
~ Cook at medium heat for about 5 minutes per side till crisp and a deep golden brown (to say the least!).
~ Sprinkle with caster sugar to serve.

Another version of Welsh Cakes, Llech Cymraeg, are often made with wholemeal flour, and no raising agent. This makes a much crisper cake.

Sussex Plum Heavies

I am confused – dried plums are prunes, aren't they? Why then, does every recipe I have ever seen for Plum Heavies contain currants and not prunes? Soft brown sugar is a good alternative in these.

1 x key recipe BUT using 50% lard and 50% butter
110g/4oz currants
a little milk for glazing

~ Preheat the oven to 200°C/400°F/180C fan/gas 6.
~ When making the dough rub in the lard but not the butter.
~ Stir in the sugar and currants and then enough milk to make a soft workable dough.
~ Roll the dough out to a rough rectangle.
~ Cut half the butter into small pieces and dot over the dough.
~ Fold it in three (letter fold), re-roll and repeat with the rest of the butter.

- ~ Roll out a little thinner than usual, cut into rounds.
- ~ Brush with milk and bake for about 15 minutes till golden.

Lardy Johns also from Sussex (aka Figgie Hobbins in Cornwall)

A little meagre I feel but nevertheless they deserve a place here.

1 x key recipe with the following provisos ...
the fat should be lard
the liquid should be water
50g/2oz currants

- ~ Preheat the oven to 200°C/400°F/180C fan/gas 6.
- ~ Make the key recipe with the changes listed above.
- ~ Roll the dough out to a rectangle about 1.5cm/½" thick and cut into 5cm/2"squares.
- ~ As usual lay on a lightly greased baking tray and cook for about 15 minutes till golden.
- ~ Eat warm with butter and/or jam.

Fat Rascals from Yorkshire

These are a modern-ish variation of traditional turf cakes which were baked in a covered pan in the ashes of the fire. I have recently read that turf cakes are now considered to be an endangered species!

This version is cooked in the oven.

1 x key recipe BUT replace the milk with ...
1 egg beaten with 2 tablespoons milk
the finely grated zest of half an orange
the finely grated zest of half a lemon
½ teaspoon ground cinnamon
¼ teaspoon ground nutmeg
75g/3oz mixed dried fruit
1 egg yolk beaten with 1 teaspoon water and a pinch of salt – to glaze
a few slivered almonds and glacé cherries to decorate

- ~ Preheat the oven to 200°C/400°F/180C fan/gas 6.
- ~ Prepare the dough adding the zests, spices and fruits together with the sugar.
- ~ Mix to a soft dough with the egg and milk.
- ~ Divide into 6-8 portions, roll into balls and place on a lightly greased baking tray.
- ~ Brush with the egg and water mixture.
- ~ Decorate with almonds and cherries.

- Bake for about 15 minutes till risen and golden with hollow sounding bottoms!
- Serve warm with butter and a nice cuppa tea.

Devonshire Apple Dappy

They might jam and cream their scones in the wrong order in Devonshire but they make a totally wonderful apple dessert using our key recipe dough.

> finely grated zest and juice of 1 lemon
> 1 tablespoon Golden Syrup or Honey
> 40g/1½oz butter
> 4 tablespoons sugar
> 100ml/3½ fl oz water
> 4 apples
> 1x key recipe
> 2 tablespoons light brown sugar

- Preheat the oven to 190 °C/375°F/170°C fan/ gas 5.
- Butter a shallow ovenproof dish.
- Bring the first 4 ingredients to a boil stirring to melt the butter and sugar then simmer for a couple of minutes. Set aside.
- Make the dough and roll out to a rectangle about 1¼cm/½" thick.
- Peel and coarsely chop the apples and toss with the light brown sugar.
- Sprinkle the sugary apples over the dough and roll up, Swiss roll style, starting from a long edge.
- Cut the roll into thick slices and arrange, cut sides up, in the greased dish.
- Pour over the syrup and bake till risen, crusty, golden and sticky – 30-35 minutes.

Serve with custard, cream, ice cream or, best of all, clotted cream.

~ *Cobblers, Slumps & Similar* ~

There are several dishes of this type that can be made using the key recipe but I'm not quite sure how many! The thing is the same recipe will go under several names or, equally confusing, one name will sometimes apply to more than one dish. There is even something called a Sonker but research has revealed that nobody really knows quite what it is!

Here are some ideas – call them what you like!

Cobblers

A cobbler is a sweet or savoury filling topped with soft scone rounds so that it resembles a cobbled street, apparently. As an example …

Plum Cobbler

900g/2lb stoned and quartered plums
110g/4oz caster sugar
1 x key recipe made with soft light brown sugar
a little more milk and sugar

~ Toss together the plums and sugar and set aside in a shallow ovenproof dish whilst you prepare the dough.
~ Preheat the oven to 190 °C/375°F/170°C fan/gas 5.
~ Make the dough as usual.
~ EITHER pinch off small quantities of dough and arrange attractively over the fruit OR roll out, cut into pretty shapes and lay them on top of the fruit OR make a soft dough and dollop it onto the fruit.
~ Brush dough with a little milk and sprinkle with sugar.
~ Bake for 30-35 minutes or so till the crust is risen and golden and the fruit is cooked.

If you prefer and especially with longer cooking fruits such as apples – part cook them before topping with the cobbles.

Savoury cobblers work well too – try a rich beef stew topped with cheddar scones, lamb stew with garlic and rosemary scones, a fish pie version with lemon and herb scones and so on.

Slumps aka Grunts

Seemingly these are the same thing from different parts of the States. They are similar to a cobbler but the dough is made into dumplings and cooked on top of the stove.

See page 50 for information about doughnuts and how to cook them.

Pandowdy

This too is similar to a cobbler but the dough is rolled thinner, placed on top of the dish in one piece and then – and this makes a change – when baked and almost ready to serve the crust is broken and some, but by no means all, is pushed under the surface of the filling to produce a mix of crisp and soggy topping.

Apple Pandowdy is the norm but here is a Blackberry and Apple version.

~ *Short & Crumbly* ~

This splendid dough can also be rolled a little thinner and used as a crust – upper, lower, both or neither! It is very short and crumbly so fragile when handling but if you do mess up a bit and make a hole, just smidge a bit of dough over to mend it. Rustic!

Tarts

To Bake Blind

~ Preheat the oven to 200°C/400°F/180C fan/gas 6.
~ As with normal pastry, roll the dough out quite thinly, say 5mm/¼", and use to line a greased tart case or cases. Loose bottom ones are best.
~ Lightly prick the base of the tart several times with a fork.
~ Gently and loosely line the tart with foil and then weight it down with a layer of rice or dried beans.
~ Bake for 15 minutes, remove the foil and weighting and cook for another 5 minutes or so to dry out the base.
~ Cool on a rack.

Of course you can use anything you fancy to fill these tarts but do make sure your filling is already cooked as they cases only need a brief time in the oven to heat through.

Rustic Tarts

These are sometimes known as galettes, certain crêpes are also sometimes called galettes – it's all a bit confusing. This is a really easy way to make a tart.

~ Preheat the oven to 200°C/400°F/180C fan/gas 6.
~ Roll the dough out to about 5mm/¼" thick into a reasonably neat circle, square or rectangle.
~ Arrange your filling (which should be something fast cooking or already cooked and not too wet) on the dough leaving a border of about 2½cm/1".
~ Fold the edge up and over to frame the filling.
~ Bake for 15-20 minutes till the edge is crisp and golden and the filling hot through.

Tarte Tatin

For the uninitiated a Tarte Tatin is a kind of upside down tart. It's a bit like a pie with the filling baked under a crust BUT, cunningly, when ready the pie is turned out filling side up thus resulting in a crispy bottom and a caramelised top. Puff pastry is commonly used but scone dough make a great alternative. As an example …

Caramelised Shallot Tatin with Blue Cheese Crust

450g/1lb shallots – peeled
a little olive oil and a little butter
salt and pepper
a splash of red wine
1 x key recipe made with blue cheese (see page 20)

~ Shallots when peeled separate into two or three bulbs, if necessary halve any big ones so that they all of similar size.
~ Heat together the butter and oil and slowly cook the shallots till beautifully browned.
~ If they are not quite tender once coloured to your liking put a lid on the pan and continue to cook very gently till they are.
~ Add a splash of red wine and continue to cook, without the lid, shaking the pan till a glaze has formed on the shallots.
~ Preheat the oven to 200°C/400°F/180C fan/gas 6.
~ Arrange the shallots in one layer in an ovenproof dish bearing in mind that when you turn the tatin out the bottom of the shallots will be on the top so make them pretty.
~ Roll out the dough very slightly larger than the size and the shape of your dish.
~ Cover the shallots with the pastry tucking it in around the edges.
~ Bake till the pastry is risen and crisp.
~ Cool for a few minutes then turn out carefully.

Pies

In short – just replace the crust in your favourite pie with the basic dough, flavoured appropriately and rolled out to about 5mm/¼" (or thicker if you like). This is an ideal chance to go a bit Yorkshire; how about a delicious apple pie with a Cheddar Crust?

Turnovers

Of course our dough can be folded around a filling to completely enclose it and to be honest I think I prefer it to normal pastry; lovely and short!

Make sure the filling is cold and not too wet or the turnover might fall apart whilst cooking. Bake at 200°C/400°F/180C fan/gas 6.

These contain butternut squash roasted with red onion and chorizo - just because I had some, turnovers are a great way to use up leftovers!

Biscuits of the English Persuasion

1 x key recipe
2 tablespoons caster sugar

~ Preheat the oven to 200°C/400°F/180C fan/gas 6.
~ On a lightly floured surface roll the dough out pretty thinly.
~ Lift the dough from the board (this is easily done by draping it over the rolling pin) and sprinkle the surface with the caster sugar.
~ Roll the dough out a little more on the sugar – one side only, do not turn the dough.
~ Cut into pretty shapes.
~ Lay sugar side up on an ungreased baking tray and bake for 8-10 minutes till lightly golden on top.
~ Cool on a rack – serve with coffee, creamy desserts or ice cream.

Suggestions ...

~ Try flavoured sugars such as cinnamon or vanilla for extra deliciousness.
~ Add grated orange or lemon zest to the dough.
~ Mix in a little ground cinnamon or ginger.
~ Drizzle with icing or dip one end in melted chocolate once cooked and cooled.

Or with savoury dough ...

~ Roll onto grated Parmesan instead of flour.
~ Add herbs.
~ Season with spices, anything from black pepper to sumac or chipotle!

Crumble

If you don't add any liquid to the basic recipe you have a fine crumble topping for Apple Crumbles and similar. If you are feeling creative add coconut or oats or chopped nuts to the mix.

~ *Dumplings & Doughnuts* ~

Mince and Dumplings is one of my Geordie lad's favourite meals. I make these so often and every time I do he looks surprised and says "nice dumplings!" which is possibly the greatest compliment he has ever given me!

Dumplings

Make sure your stew is deep enough that the dumplings don't touch the bottom and wide enough that they don't touch each other. I usually make a double quantity of stew and do the dumplings for the first night when it is plentiful for dumplinging in, any leftover stew gets made into a cobbler or similar.

1 x key recipe without the sugar and with a little more salt.

~ Have your delicious stew which you have already made at a simmer before you add the milk to the basic recipe.
~ Add the milk, make the dough and roll it into walnut sized balls – makes about 14 so enough for 3-4 standard people or 1½ Geordies.
~ Drop the balls, spaced out a bit so they don't touch, into the simmering stew.
~ Turn down the heat, cover the pot and cook for about 20 minutes till the dumplings are risen and firm.
~ Take the lid off the pot and allow to steam for a couple more minutes to dry out the tops of the dumplings.

May I suggest Cheddar dumplings using the cheese dough (recipe on page 20) in a beefy stew or herby ones with chicken?

Likky Stew with a Natterjack

In the West Country (of the UK) large savoury dumplings are sometimes referred to as natterjacks, perhaps because I suppose they could possibly slightly resemble a natterjack toad, maybe!

Make a lovely thick leek soup or stew and cook 1 large (toad shaped!) dumpling in it per person! Serve immediately, swimming on top of the soup. Of course, this is a great way to serve all sorts of soups and dumplings.

Sweet Dumplings

Sometimes a dish of cooked fruit topped with sweet dumplings is called a Slump or Grunt (see page 40) and sometimes it isn't!

1 x key recipe
a deep wide pot of cooked fruit, simmering gently

~ Make the key recipe.
~ Roll the dough into walnut sized balls and drop them gently into the simmering fruit.
~ Turn down the heat, cover the pot and cook for about 20 minutes till the dumplings are risen and firm.
~ Take the lid off the pot and allow to steam for a couple more minutes to dry out the tops of the dumplings.

Grand-Père – a superb Canadian dish
serves 2-3

These are simply little dumplings simmered in diluted maple syrup. By the time they are cooked the syrup has concentrated back into a glorious sticky goo which coats the dumplings and makes you happy!

Maple syrup is quite pricey so I have also tried making these with maple flavoured syrup which worked fine too. (Probably honey or golden syrup would also work but would not be authentic.)

1 x key recipe
350ml/12 fl oz each of maple syrup and water
chopped pecans – optional
clotted cream – optional but you'd be mad not to!

~ Bring the water and syrup to a fast simmer in a pan, with a lid, that is broad enough to allow the dumplings to swell without touching.
~ Make the dough and roll into 2cm/¾" balls.
~ Gently drop the dumplings into the simmering syrup, turn down the heat and put the lid on.
~ Simmer for about 10 minutes till risen and firm when gently poked.
~ Lift gently onto plates, sprinkle with chopped pecans and dollop with clotted cream.
~ Eat immediately.

Incidentally the dumplings do tend to sink and stick on the pan a little as the liquid is not thick enough to float them. Just ease them off gently when cooked.

Doughnuts

Playing about with my dough one afternoon I had a small piece left over and wondered what would happen if I deep fried it. Much to my delight I found myself, a few minutes later enjoying a cup of coffee and a hot sugary doughnut!

1 x key recipe or any sweet scone dough
innocuous tasting oil
a bowl of sugar (could be flavoured eg. cinnamon or vanilla sugar as appropriate)

~ If you don't have a deep fryer (I don't) then put enough oil in a deep saucepan to allow the doughnuts to easily float BUT, and this is important, DO NOT fill the pot more than one third full or there is a danger it might overflow which is both messy and very dangerous.
~ Start heating the oil to 190° C /375° F before making the dough.
~ Make the dough whilst the oil is heating.
~ Form the dough into walnut sized balls or just pinch off lumps and when the oil comes to temperature deep fry them till golden all over – about 5 minutes.
~ Lift out carefully and drain on kitchen roll.
~ Roll in the bowl of sugar and serve warm or cold.

As you can see from the picture I popped a (slightly off centre) nugget of chocolate in the middle of my doughnuts before frying – no reason why you shouldn't do the same!

Incidentally I understand that this sort of thing, in Australia, is known as a Puftaloon – how lovely!

Savoury Doughnuts

Although less common doughnuts can also be savoury and are easily made using any appropriate version of this dough. Here are some ideas …

~ Lemon and herb doughnuts filled with flaked crab mixed with a little cream cheese.
~ Cheddar doughnuts rolled in freshly grated parmesan after frying.
~ Bacon doughnuts with a maple syrup drizzle.
~ Sour cream and green onion (just chop the green part of spring onions and mix into the sour cream dough).
~ Any ideas?

~ *Leftovers!* ~

I love cooking with leftovers, they are my favourite ingredient. I can pretty well always think of something good to do with any bits, pieces and trimmings.

Dough Trimmings ...

After cutting out your scones you may be left with scraps of dough which *must not be wasted.*

~ Make yourself a miniature cook's treat or tester; a baby scone, rock cake or maybe a little jam thumbprint, because you're worth it!
~ Roll the dough out thinly, sprinkle or spread with something (brown sugar, chopped nuts, jam or, if savoury, cheese and bacon or similar), roll up, slice and bake pinwheels.
~ Make a few English type biscuits – see page 45
~ The cheese dough makes splendid cheese straws.

Leftover Scones and Similar ...

~ Scones, rock cakes etc. make pleasant toast. Serve with lots of butter.
~ They can also be crumbled, sautéed in butter till crisp and sprinkled over ice cream.
~ Or this is a good idea ....

Scone and (no) Butter Pudding!

about 100g/3½oz leftover scones
200ml/7 fl oz milk
100ml/3½ fl oz double cream
2 eggs
80g/3oz sugar
½ teaspoon vanilla essence
a little extra sugar

~ Slice the scones and arrange in a buttered ovenproof dish or divide between ramekins.
~ Whisk together all the other ingredients (except the extra sugar) and pour over the scones pushing any bits sticking out under the surface to soak.
~ Set aside from 30 minutes up to several hours.
~ Preheat oven to 180°C/350°F/160°C fan/gas 4.

~   Sprinkle the pudding with the extra sugar and bake for about 40 minutes till risen, golden and slightly wobbly when nudged.

Serve hot, warm or cold but warm is best.

Various things can, of course, be added to this – try dried fruit, alcoholic dried fruit (page 56), fresh fruit, lumps of chocolate etc.

Leftover Dumplings

Leftover dumplings fry up a treat, in fact when I used to put dumplings on the menu they were always fried as cooking fresh to order is a bugger when busy. Also they are delicious this way, maybe better than un-fried!

I like to cut dumplings in half first to give a good flat area to go crisp but cut or not fry them in a little oil till hot, crisp and crunchy. Serve with stew, soup or sauce of your choice. Here are some reclining in a bowl of spicy tomato soup with a little parmesan.

~ 5 Ancillary Recipes ~

Sticky Toffee Sauce

This is unctuous and great on all sorts of things including Sticky Toffee Pudding. It keeps well, rewarm to use.

125g/4½ oz butter
225g/8oz soft dark brown sugar
1 teaspoon vanilla essence
175ml/6 fl oz double (heavy) cream

~ Melt together the butter and dark brown sugar, stirring all the time.
~ Add the vanilla essence and the cream and stir in completely then bring to a fast simmer but do not boil.
~ Remove from heat and use or cool and save in the fridge till needed.

Handy hint – the sauce may separate when re-warming in which case just stir in a tad of cold cream and it will re-emulsify and be as gorgeous as ever.

Alcohol Soaked Fruit

Put some dried fruit into a clean sterilised jam jar and pour in enough spirit, golden rum or brandy are my favourites, to cover completely. I haven't given quantities here as you can make as much as you like. The fruit keeps, improving all the time, almost forever, provided you make sure it is always covered with alcohol. You can use it in all sorts of ways including spooning it into your mouth whilst standing in the kitchen. You must, however, leave it alone for at least 24 hours.

Drops Scones as we normally understand them!

This makes about 8 x 2"/5cm drop scones

> 125g/4½oz plain flour
> a pinch of salt
> 1 tablespoon sugar
> rounded teaspoon baking powder
> 1 egg
> 100ml/3½ fl oz milk
> a little vegetable oil

~ Stir together the first 4 ingredients.
~ Male a well in the middle of the flour mixture.
~ Break the egg into the well.
~ Gently whisk the egg into the flour and, as it thickens, gradually add the milk, still whisking, till you have a thick but pourable batter. This may or may not take all the milk, or might even need a tad more, depending on the make and age of the flour.
~ Heat a non-stick frying pan and carefully, using a piece of paper towel, smear the surface with a little cooking oil.
~ When the pan is hot and greasy pour a 5cm/2" circle of batter in the pan and cook till the surface is pitted with burst bubble holes.
~ Using a spatula or a deft flip of the wrist turn the pancake and cook till the other side is golden.

Serve immediately with butter and or honey or go a bit exotic and have maple syrup and bacon.

Sausage Gravy!

350g/12oz pork sausages
2 tablespoons flour
475ml/16 fl oz milk
freshly ground black pepper

~ Remove the skins from the sausages and pull the meat into little pieces.
~ Cook the pieces in a hot pan till cooked, 5-6 minutes, then remove with a slotted spoon and set aside.
~ Add the flour to the sausage fat left in the pan and stir in to make a roux (paste). Cook gently, stirring over low heat for a minute or so.
~ Whisk in the milk till smooth and thick then simmer for a couple of minutes.
~ Stir in the reserved sausagemeat.
~ Taste and season, especially with pepper.
~ Serve with warm American Biscuits (aka scones!), preferably made with buttermilk.

How to Roast Garlic

~ Preheat the oven to 190°C/375°F/170°C fan/gas 5.
~ Cut heads of garlic in half through their equators and stand cut sides up in a shallow ovenproof dish.
~ Drizzle quite generously with olive oil, being sure to anoint the cut surfaces well, and season with salt and pepper.
~ Cover tightly with foil and bake till completely tender which takes about an hour, it is ready when lightly golden and buttery soft.
~ Cool till you are able to handle it and then squeeze the soft garlic cloves into a clean jar (or some scone dough!) adding any oil remaining in the dish too.
~ Pour in extra olive oil to cover the garlic completely, put on the lid and store in the fridge till needed.

~ *Summing Up* ~

I think that's about all I can think of to tell you!

Now you have a go!

Thank you so much for reading this, I hope you enjoyed it and all the wonderful things you will make.

Good reviews are important to a book's success these days. If you enjoyed this book (or indeed any book by anyone) please take the time to review it on Amazon. Just a few lines will be a real help and I'll be very grateful!

Suzy Bowler

~ Index ~

Adding Additions 4
Alcohol Soaked Fruit 56
American Biscuits 9
Apples …
    Caramelised Apple Scones 13
    Devonshire Apple Dappy 38

Bake Blind, how to 43
Banana, Caramel Shortcakes 29
Biscuits …
    American 9
    English 45
Black Garlic Scones 22
Blueberry Scones, Sautéed 13
Caramel …
    Caramelised Apple Scones 13
    Caramel-Banana Shortcakes 29
    Caramelised Onion Scones 21
    Caramelised Shallot Tatin with Blue Cheese Crust 44

Caribbean Coconut Rock Cakes 33

Cheese …
    Caramelised Shallot Tatin with Blue Cheese Crust 44
    Cheese Scones 20
Chilli, Dark Chocolate Rock Cakes 32

Chocolate …
    Chocolate Scones 16
    Dark Chocolate (and Chilli) Rock Cakes
    Dried Cherry & White Chocolate Rock Cakes 32
Clotted Cream 8
Cobblers 40
Coconut Rock Cakes, Caribbean 33
Cranberry Orange Scones 12
Cream Teas 8
Crumble 46
Dark Chocolate (and Chilli) Rock Cakes 32
Devonshire Apple Dappy 38
Dough trimmings 53
Doughnuts 50
    Savoury Doughnuts 51
Dried Cherry & White Chocolate Rock Cakes 32
Drop Scones …
    Drops Scones as we normally understand them! 56
    Not Quite Drop Scones 26
Dumplings 48
    Grand-Père 49
    Leftovers 54
    Likky Stew with a Natterjack 49
    Sweet Dumplings 49

Fat Rascals   37

Fats   4

Figgie Hobbins   37

Filled Scones   18

Flatbreads   27

Flours   3

Freezing   7

Fruit and Nut Rock Cakes,
   Fully Loaded   32

Fruit Scones, Traditional   11

Garlic Bread Scones   22

Garlic …
   Black Garlic Scones   22
   Garlic Bread Scones   22
   How to Roast   57
   Roasted Garlic Scones   22

GENIUS RECIPE   2

Gingerbread Rock Cakes   33

Girdle Scones   26

Glazes   7

Golden Syrup Scones   14

Grand-Père   49

Griddle Scones   26

Grunts   40

Herb Scones   21

Honey Scones   14

Hot Cross Scones   11

How to Roast Garlic   57

Important Points   6

Lardy Johns   37

Leftovers …
   Dough   53
   Dumplings   54
   Scones and Similar   53

Lemon Poppy Seed Scones   14

Likky Cakes   21

Likky Stew with a Natterjack   49

Liquids   5

Maple Syrup Scones   14

Monkey Scones!   17

Mushrooms Scones   23

Northumbrian Singin' Hinnies   35

Not Quite Drop Scones!   26

Onions …
   Caramelised Onion Scones   21
   Caramelised Shallot Tatin with
      Blue Cheese Crust   44

Orange …
   Cranberry Orange Scones   12
   Sticky Orange Buns   16

Pandowdy   41

Panko Crusted Balls   24

Peanut Butter Scones   15

Pecan and Brown Sugar Scones   15

Pice ar y maen   36

Pies   44

Plum Cobbler   40

Plum Heavies, Sussex   36

Puftaloon 51

Pumpkin Scones 21

Roasted Garlic Scones 22

Roasted Tomato Scones 24

Rock Buns/Cakes 31

    Traditional Rock Cakes 32
    Fully Loaded Fruit and Nut Rock Cakes 32
    Dried Cherry & White Chocolate Rock Cakes 32
    Dark Chocolate (and Chilli) Rock Cakes 32
    Caribbean Coconut Rock Cakes 33
    Gingerbread Rock Cakes 33

Rubbing In 3

Rum & Raisin Scones 11

Rustic Tarts 43

Sandwich Scones 18

Sausage Gravy! 57

Sautéed Blueberry Scones 13

Savoury Doughnuts 51

Scone and (no) Butter Pudding 53

Shallot Tatin with Blue Cheese Crust, Caramelised 44

Shortcakes 29

    Almost Classic Strawberry Shortcake 29
    Caramel-Banana Shortcakes 29
    Tomato Shortcakes 30

Singin' Hinnies 35

Slumps 40

Sonker 39

Sticky Orange Buns 16

Sticky Toffee Sauce 55

Sticky Toffee Scones 15

Storage 7

Strawberries & Cream Scones 12

Strawberry Shortcake 29

Sussex Plum Heavies 36

Sweet Dumplings 49

Sweet Potato Scones 21

Tarte Tatin 44

Tarts 43

Tomato Shortcakes 30

Toppings 7

Traditional Rock Cakes 32

Treacle Scones 14

Turnovers 45

Welsh Cakes 36

Printed in Poland
by Amazon Fulfillment
Poland Sp. z o.o., Wrocław